# Customer Service Skills Profile

Dr. Jon Warner

**HRD Press • Amherst • Massachusetts**

Published by:    HRD Press, Inc.
                 22 Amherst Road
                 Amherst, MA 01002
                 (800) 822-2801 (U.S. and Canada)
                 (413) 253-3488
                 (413) 253-3490 (Fax)
                 http://www.hrdpress.com

In association with Team Publications.

ISBN: 0-87425-840-5

Cover design by Eileen Klockars
Production services by Anctil Virtual Office

# Introduction and Instructions

Most customers are willing to pay a premium to have their basic needs met in a timely and efficient manner, and will be pleasantly surprised (and grateful) if they are treated with a little dignity and respect in the bargain. This isn't asking for much, but consistent, responsive, and respectful treatment is surprisingly hard to come by.

Best-practice organizations do not want customers to be surprised when they get good service. It's not good enough. Instead, they work hard to ensure that every moment of truth or interface point with a customer creates a good impression. They achieve this by making sure that each person who serves customers directly and each person on the internal staff who serves the frontline staff is competent in a range of important service skills.

Which service skills or competencies are most critical in customer service? There are several key themes or broad competencies that seem to be priorities for good service providers. Extensive industry research suggests that there are seven competency areas. These are:

- **Temperament/Disposition**
- **Attentive Listening**
- **Communicating Clearly**
- **Resolving Conflict**
- **Engaging in Joint Problem Solving**
- **Carefully Negotiating**
- **Building Warmth and Empathy**

This instrument has been designed as a self-scoring customer service skills assessment that will help individuals understand more about their relative competence in this critical area. The seven competencies that constitute outstanding service are assessed individually and collectively in order to come up with the individual's overall profile.

The competency areas can be considered as separate sets of skills, but together they create a kind of Service Skills jigsaw puzzle. No one piece will supply you with all the skills you need. By aspiring to improve your performance in all of these competencies, you can improve your ability to provide the kind of service customers want, need, and expect to pay for.

Each of these competency areas is defined and explained briefly on the assessment page.

# Completing this Booklet

This questionnaire will be easy to complete. Read each introductory paragraph to understand the competency, and then select a response from 1–5. Shade in all the boxes below the number you marked. You will be creating a bar graph or "histogram" to give you a quick visual reference of your scores.

**Example:** Score = 3

| 1 | 2 | 3 | 4 | 5 |
|---|---|---|---|---|
| ■ | ■ | ■ |   |   |

The scale for each competency will always be 1–5, extending from "almost never" or 1 on the left to "almost always" or 5 on the right. Once all 12 questions in the section have been answered, you will be able to draw conclusions about how skilled you presently are in customer service.

As a final step, add up all of your scores and divide them by 12 (the total number of questions). Shade in the total score box the same way. This time, you will get an exact score (like 3.7). It's okay to shade in part of a box here, if necessary.

After you have shaded the response boxes, look at the interpretation notes at the bottom of the page. These notes will explain the likely impact of certain scores and suggest ways to improve weak areas. Be sure you read the notes for all eight competencies (one on each page).

After you have completed and read the interpretation notes for all eight competency areas, turn to page 11 and plot your category scores on the "spider" diagram. Once you have connected all of the points, you will create your overall Customer Service Skills profile. Then add up all the individual scores from all the competency areas and divide by 7. Enter your total "Customer Service Skills" score in the box provided.

Pages 11 and 12 provide some further general notes on action that can be taken to improve weak areas.

The Personal Action Plan checklist provided on page 14 will help individuals develop a written plan to address some of the items and issues identified by the assessment. Copy this page and give it to a friend or family member, and ask them to check (after 3 months or so) whether or not you have implemented/are implementing your improvement plan.

This booklet is yours to complete and keep as a reference document. Remember, your overall profile is likely to change over time. What you fill in about yourself today may not apply in three, six, or twelve months' time. However, if you are honest with yourself, this profile will serve as an accurate picture of your overall ability to provide effective customer service and help you identify where you should concentrate your efforts to improve. You can fill out another assessment in the future to see how far you have progressed.

# Temperament/Disposition

**Temperament/Disposition refers to an individual's internal desire to derive value and enjoyment from their relationships with other people. This competency area is all about developing an open, give-and-take attitude toward people in general and customers in particular.**

Please complete this part of the questionnaire as honestly as possible. It can help you improve your ability to serve customers more effectively (if you feel this represents an accurate picture). The choice scales are as follows:

**1 = almost never; 2 = occasionally; 3 = frequently; 4 = very frequently; 5 = almost always**

Fill in all the boxes up to the score you select so you create a shaded bar.

| | Almost Never | | | | Almost Always |
|---|---|---|---|---|---|
| | 1 | 2 | 3 | 4 | 5 |
| 1. I introduce myself confidently when I meet a new person. | | | | | |
| 2. I believe that giving is better than receiving. | | | | | |
| 3. Effective service is about giving and sharing. | | | | | |
| 4. I am generally a cheerful person. | | | | | |
| 5. I am at ease in groups of people. | | | | | |
| 6. I notice how others are feeling. | | | | | |
| 7. I am good at empathizing with people. | | | | | |
| 8. Harmony and friendship are important to me. | | | | | |
| 9. I try to be reliable and sincere in order to build trust. | | | | | |
| 10. I don't mind making "small talk." | | | | | |
| 11. I care about people. | | | | | |
| 12. I believe that relationships help us grow and develop as individuals. | | | | | |

(Add up all the column scores and divide by 12) **TOTAL SCORE**

## HIGH

Scores predominantly in the fours and fives ("almost always" and "very frequently") suggest that this individual is easygoing and flexible and likes to work with and through people on a regular basis. He or she is likely to freely offer support and help and is open to sharing personal concerns and challenges, particularly when in need of advice and support.

A high scorer is likely to go out of his or her way to develop relationships with a wide range of people, offering support to them as well as appreciating the opportunity relationships provide for personal growth and learning. Many of their relationships will be deep and long-lasting friendships based on a spirit of giving and sharing.

## LOW

Scores predominantly in the ones and twos ("occasionally" and "almost never") suggest that this individual is basically a loner, doing much more by themselves than with and through other people. He or she is also likely to be selective about who they talk to, and tends to only communicate if there is a specific reason to initiate contact.

A low scorer is likely to lack general confidence about meeting or dealing with new people and will tend to keep to themselves. This individual is likely to consider most relationships to be "transactional" or only for the purpose of making an exchange of some kind on a like-for-like basis, rather than for mutual support and help.

## ACTION FOR LOW SCORERS

Low scorers need to find ways to feel more comfortable simply talking to people and ways to become more open to accepting personal feedback, support, and help. It is not easy to change quickly, but low scorers will find it helpful to try to see things from the other person's point of view, and should do things that will increase their empathy for others.

# Attentive Listening

**Attentive Listening refers to an individual's ability to hear and understand other people, and to quickly discover their full communication or message. This competency area is all about listening attentively in order to gain understanding and help the communicator successfully convey what they think and feel.**

Please complete this part of the questionnaire as honestly as possible. It can help you improve your ability to serve customers more effectively (if you feel this represents an accurate picture). The choice scales are as follows:

**1 = almost never; 2 = occasionally; 3 = frequently; 4 = very frequently; 5 = almost always**

Fill in all the boxes up to the score you select so you create a shaded bar.

| | Almost Never | | | | Almost Always |
|---|---|---|---|---|---|
| | 1 | 2 | 3 | 4 | 5 |
| 1. I give people my complete attention when they are speaking. | | | | | |
| 2. I create a positive climate where people can be candid with me. | | | | | |
| 3. I let people share their views and opinions before offering my own. | | | | | |
| 4. I create a warm and relaxed atmosphere for people to talk openly. | | | | | |
| 5. I avoid jumping into a conversation to take control. | | | | | |
| 6. I am calm and patient during discussions with customers. | | | | | |
| 7. I listen to understand, rather than to reply. | | | | | |
| 8. I observe body language as well as listen to the words. | | | | | |
| 9. I often paraphrase what is said in conversations. | | | | | |
| 10. I am focused and patient when people talk to me. | | | | | |
| 11. I avoid interrupting or finishing other people's sentences. | | | | | |
| 12. I listen to the overall message or key theme being expressed. | | | | | |

(Add up all the column scores and divide by 12) **TOTAL SCORE**

## HIGH

Scores predominantly in the fours and fives ("almost always" and "very frequently") suggest that this individual recognizes the value of giving focused, concentrated attention to what customers are communicating. He or she tends to look for the best possible climate for people to talk, lets them speak without interruption, and then carefully assesses what is being said.

A high scorer is likely to quickly demonstrate that he or she values what people have to say, and shows patience and a suitable temperament for offering people guidance in relation to their feedback, requests, or concerns. By trying to create a quiet, warm, and easy atmosphere for conversation, high scorers develop a reputation for being highly receptive and for providing welcoming service.

## LOW

Scores predominantly in the ones and twos ("occasionally" and "almost never") suggest that this individual is unlikely to give their full attention to customers offering feedback, requests, or concerns, focusing more on what they want to say than on understanding the customer. They generally choose an inappropriate listening climate, interrupt people before they finish speaking, and let their mind wander off track.

A low scorer is someone customers tend to avoid contact with because they do not believe their feedback will be fully valued or used to resolve the problem. Low scorers often give the impression that they are impatient and distracted, and therefore have only limited time to offer good service or support.

## ACTION FOR LOW SCORERS

Low scorers need to become more-attentive listeners by giving much more of their time and attention to others when they are speaking with them (in all but the shortest conversations). They can start to do this by maintaining good eye contact, not interrupting, paraphrasing and summarizing what they hear, and making the effort to understand all of what the speaker is trying to convey.

# Communicating Clearly

**Communicating Clearly refers to an individual's efforts to speak clearly, warmly, and understandably with each customer. This competency area is all about making yourself understood when communicating with all kinds of people.**

Please complete this part of the questionnaire as honestly as possible. It can help you improve your ability to serve customers more effectively (if you feel this represents an accurate picture). The choice scales are as follows:

**1 = almost never; 2 = occasionally; 3 = frequently; 4 = very frequently; 5 = almost always**

Fill in all the boxes up to the score you select so you create a shaded bar.

| | Almost Never | | | | Almost Always |
|---|---|---|---|---|---|
| | 1 | 2 | 3 | 4 | 5 |
| 1. I listen to customers' issues and concerns to help shape my own communications. | | | | | |
| 2. I think about and carefully shape the way I communicate complex information. | | | | | |
| 3. I use multiple channels to get my messages across to customers. | | | | | |
| 4. I am very aware of the needs of each "audience"—individuals as well as groups. | | | | | |
| 5. I ask as many questions as are necessary to get a clear view of what is possible. | | | | | |
| 6. I use clear, simple language to describe action steps. | | | | | |
| 7. I openly give and receive feedback. | | | | | |
| 8. I am usually good at reading other people. | | | | | |
| 9. I flex my communication style and method when necessary for clarity. | | | | | |
| 10. I am generally patient and give customers plenty of time to ask questions. | | | | | |
| 11. I try to find the right words for the circumstances. | | | | | |
| 12. I translate the core message in as many ways as necessary to create complete understanding. | | | | | |

(Add up all the column scores and divide by 12) **TOTAL SCORE**

## HIGH

Scores predominantly in the fours and fives ("almost always" and "very frequently") suggest that this individual thinks carefully about the channels that he or she uses to transmit a message and the most appropriate way to communicate it. To do this, he or she tries hard to always be clear, concise, and consistent in what is said or done.

A high scorer is likely to be acutely aware of their power to communicate and influence customers through good preparation, audience needs analysis, and a versatility of communication methods designed to ensure that every customer they have contact with is given the best opportunity to understand the message.

## LOW

Scores predominantly in the ones and twos ("occasionally" and "almost never") suggest that this individual tends to ignore or forget the needs of different customer groups. They are not likely to select the most appropriate communication channels, and in fact tend to use only one communication or delivery style, regardless of the situation).

A low scorer is likely to find communication challenging and perhaps even taxing—something to get over and done with as quickly as possible. Communicating his or her message is likely to be a chore. This attitude affects their understanding and consequently their actions.

## ACTION FOR LOW SCORERS

Low scorers need to think more about the variety of customer preferences in terms of receiving information and how different channels and styles can affect how well a particular message is understood. Low scorers should do a better job listening to customer feedback, and adapt their communication style and content appropriately to maximize clarity and understanding.

# Resolving Conflict

**Resolving Conflict refers to how well an individual deals with a customer's irritation and any resultant conflict or concern surrounding the issue. This competency area is all about adopting a positive, constructive, and solution-focused approach whenever conflict arises.**

Please complete this part of the questionnaire as honestly as possible. It can help you improve your ability to serve customers more effectively (if you feel this represents an accurate picture). The choice scales are as follows:

**1 = almost never; 2 = occasionally; 3 = frequently; 4 = very frequently; 5 = almost always**

Fill in all the boxes up to the score you select so you create a shaded bar.

| | Almost Never | | | | Almost Always |
|---|---|---|---|---|---|
| | 1 | 2 | 3 | 4 | 5 |
| 1. I try to calm things down when discussions get a little heated. | | | | | |
| 2. I handle interpersonal conflict with tact and finesse. | | | | | |
| 3. I try to keep discussions issue-oriented and blame-free when conflict arises. | | | | | |
| 4. I manage interpersonal conflict maturely and constructively. | | | | | |
| 5. I am open to and accepting of constructive criticism of any kind. | | | | | |
| 6. I handle tough people and strong personalities with confidence and composure. | | | | | |
| 7. I try to attack problems, not people. | | | | | |
| 8. I maintain my composure, even when others lose theirs. | | | | | |
| 9. I quickly resolve miscommunication problems with customers. | | | | | |
| 10. I find common ground to help people resolve differences. | | | | | |
| 11. I try to resolve conflict so that there are no losers. | | | | | |
| 12. I learn from my mistakes in dealing with conflict, and I apply new learning flexibly. | | | | | |

(Add up all the column scores and divide by 12) **TOTAL SCORE**

## HIGH

Scores predominantly in the fours and fives ("almost always" and "very frequently") suggest that the individual deals reasonably with conflict whenever it arises, calming the situation down, maintaining composure (even in the face of aggressive comments and body language), and focusing on the issue at hand (rather than the emotional components associated with the customer's antagonism).

A high scorer is likely to quickly steer the conversation toward a sensible and constructive exchange, and then try to attack the problem that the customer has identified with tact and diplomacy. The effective service provider tries to learn from each conflict situation so he or she can become even more adept at resolving disputes.

## LOW

Scores predominantly in the ones and twos ("occasionally" and "almost never") suggest that this individual finds conflict personally difficult and even stressful. He or she is likely to become overly emotional in a conflict situation, rather than immediately look for ways to address the real underlying issues that caused the conflict to occur.

A low scorer is likely to want to run away from the conflict situation or to concede important points or even become overly argumentative or stubborn, perhaps irritating the customer even further. In some conflict situations, low scorers tend to engage in too many personal or emotional exchanges and thus fail to reach an acceptable conclusion satisfactory to both sides.

## ACTION FOR LOW SCORERS

Low scorers need to think carefully about their own conflict-handling style and learn to separate themselves (personally and emotionally) from the facts and issues that have caused the conflict (typically failures in systems). Low scorers should also practice how to calm upset customers and find ways to get the customer to focus on the facts and the action steps that can sensibly resolve the issue that causes them concern.

# Engaging in Joint Problem Solving

**Engaging in Joint Problem Solving refers to an individual's efforts to find appropriate ways to analyze situations and customer concerns and suggest actions that can help resolve the problem. This competency area is all about providing customers with a useful contextual framework to think about their concerns and then guide them to a satisfactory resolution.**

Please complete this part of the questionnaire as honestly as possible. It can help you improve your ability to serve customers more effectively (if you feel this represents an accurate picture). The choice scales are as follows:

**1 = almost never; 2 = occasionally; 3 = frequently; 4 = very frequently; 5 = almost always**

Fill in all the boxes up to the score you select so you create a shaded bar.

| | Almost Never | | | | Almost Always |
|---|---|---|---|---|---|
| | 1 | 2 | 3 | 4 | 5 |
| 1. I point out that there is inevitably a new or different way to tackle most things. | | | | | |
| 2. I help people understand the facts before looking for a solution. | | | | | |
| 3. I encourage people to challenge conventional wisdom. | | | | | |
| 4. I routinely demonstrate and use a range of problem-solving methods and tools. | | | | | |
| 5. I quickly help people separate assumptions from hard evidence. | | | | | |
| 6. I make sure that apples are being compared with apples when solving problems. | | | | | |
| 7. I get people to challenge paradigms or sacred cows. | | | | | |
| 8. I help people identify several possible answers or options, not just one. | | | | | |
| 9. I try to identify the consequences of various courses of action. | | | | | |
| 10. I encourage customers to look for the context of the issue or problem. | | | | | |
| 11. I invite customers to work with me to find solutions. | | | | | |
| 12. I ask probing and incisive questions to help customers discover the real causes of problems. | | | | | |

(Add up all the column scores and divide by 12) **TOTAL SCORE**

## HIGH

Scores predominantly in the fours and fives ("almost always" and "very frequently") suggest that this individual encourages customers to look at problems or issues from different viewpoints and to use a range of different analysis tools to do so. He or she is likely to encourage them to generate several possible solutions and to carefully evaluate the one most likely to provide the best possible course of future action, based on the evidence.

A high scorer is likely to be considered suitably knowledgeable in a range of problem solving approaches and capable of suggesting the most appropriate of these, depending on the circumstances.

## LOW

Scores predominantly in the ones and twos ("occasionally" and "almost never") suggest that this individual rarely suggests creative ways to analyze and solve problems. He or she is likely to steer customers toward accepting arbitrary or constraining rules or boundaries, thus inhibiting their ability to find a better solution.

A low scorer is likely to have only limited skills to help customers look rigorously at the situations or circumstances that they face and (through careful sifting and analysis) come up with possible solutions. He or she generally lacks knowledge or appropriate understanding in how to use problem-solving tools or approaches that provide new insight and does not know how to create a different contextual framework that can help resolve the problem.

## ACTION FOR LOW SCORERS

Low scorers need to research a range of problem-solving methods that can help customers. They should also adopt a more incisive questioning approach and practice ways to get customers to look at issues in new contexts or from different viewpoints.

# Carefully Negotiating

**Carefully Negotiating refers to the skills an individual uses to work collaboratively with a customer to find solutions to requests, queries, and feedback that best meet the needs of all parties. This competency area is all about applying appropriate and effective negotiation and influencing strategies in order to create mutually beneficial outcomes.**

Please complete this part of the questionnaire as honestly as possible. It can help you improve your ability to serve customers more effectively (if you feel this represents an accurate picture). The choice scales are as follows:

**1 = almost never; 2 = occasionally; 3 = frequently; 4 = very frequently; 5 = almost always**

Fill in all the boxes up to the score you select so you create a shaded bar.

| | Almost Never | | | | Almost Always |
|---|---|---|---|---|---|
| | 1 | 2 | 3 | 4 | 5 |
| 1. I use tact and diplomacy in discussions with customers. | | | | | |
| 2. I negotiate creatively to reach the best possible outcomes. | | | | | |
| 3. I engage in negotiations in a sincere and open manner. | | | | | |
| 4. I try to carefully and constructively influence or persuade customers. | | | | | |
| 5. I keep customer negotiations calm and focused on the main issues at all times. | | | | | |
| 6. I am able to quickly find common ground, and use it as a springboard to generate options. | | | | | |
| 7. I try to be flexible and open when possible options are raised by the customer. | | | | | |
| 8. I try to share information in order to find potential areas of agreement. | | | | | |
| 9. I avoid expressing opinions and positions dogmatically. | | | | | |
| 10. I take the time to provide context before suggesting action. | | | | | |
| 11. I work hard to identify solutions in difficult situations. | | | | | |
| 12. I ask others for feedback on how to negotiate more effectively. | | | | | |

(Add up all the column scores and divide by 12) **TOTAL SCORE**

## HIGH

Scores predominantly in the fours and fives ("almost always" and "very frequently") suggest that this individual is relatively adept at using careful and tactful negotiation techniques and methods to generate possible solutions or mutually beneficial outcomes (for the customer and for the organization). He or she is able to rapidly identify areas of common ground and interest, think laterally when required to do so, and explain ideas and possible solutions persuasively.

A high scorer generally uses an open, approachable, and sincere communication style (avoiding any kind of narrow-mindedness), and keeps the conversation flowing flexibly toward a positive conclusion.

## LOW

Scores predominantly in the ones and twos ("occasionally" and "almost never") suggest that this individual does not always feel comfortable or entirely in control when negotiating or dealing with a customer. It is likely that either the customer dominates the discussion or the low scorer fails to work hard enough to generate ways to overcome apparent areas of difference.

A low scorer is likely to enter into discussions with customers with too many pre-set ideas, and hence does not always forcefully push for outcomes that are wanted by the organization. Customers are more likely to cut off the discussion before possible courses of positive action can be debated.

## ACTION FOR LOW SCORERS

Low scorers need to understand their existing negotiating style and the different styles adopted by customers, and need to learn how to "flex" styles when appropriate. Low scorers also need to learn how to use various negotiating methods and tactics (different questioning techniques, shifting conversation focus, lateral thinking, and the careful use of "if . . . then" statements, etc.).

# Building Warmth and Empathy

**Building Warmth and Empathy refers to the extent to which an individual creates a positive climate when communicating with people and demonstrates an understanding of the other person's viewpoint and feelings. This competency area is all about building a spirit of trust and sincerity in order for customers to feel that you identify with them and care about their concerns.**

Please complete this part of the questionnaire as honestly as possible. It can help you improve your ability to serve customers more effectively (if you feel this represents an accurate picture). The choice scales are as follows:

**1 = almost never; 2 = occasionally; 3 = frequently; 4 = very frequently; 5 = almost always**

Fill in all the boxes up to the score you select so you create a shaded bar.

| | Almost Never | | | | Almost Always |
|---|---|---|---|---|---|
| | 1 | 2 | 3 | 4 | 5 |
| **1.** I make myself fully available and accessible for customers. | | | | | |
| **2.** I avoid making sarcastic or critical comments about customers and their actions or ideas. | | | | | |
| **3.** I am sensitive to people's feelings. | | | | | |
| **4.** I am approachable and open to feedback. | | | | | |
| **5.** I put myself in the customer's shoes. | | | | | |
| **6.** I make sure that my actions match my words. | | | | | |
| **7.** I carefully observe what customers say and do. | | | | | |
| **8.** I follow through when I commit to something. | | | | | |
| **9.** I work hard to understand where customers are coming from. | | | | | |
| **10.** I believe that customers' feelings and emotions communicate more than their words. | | | | | |
| **11.** I am good at knowing just when customers need help or support. | | | | | |
| **12.** I can be fully trusted to keep a customer's confidence. | | | | | |

(Add up all the column scores and divide by 12) **TOTAL SCORE**

## HIGH

Scores predominantly in the fours and fives ("almost always" and "very frequently") suggest that this individual generally likes people and enjoys building strong and rewarding relationships. He or she is likely to try to sincerely understand customer issues and challenges and to quickly tune in to their underlying feelings about a subject.

A high scorer is likely to quickly gain a reputation as someone with whom customers can freely talk—a person who will keep their confidences and provide helpful and patient guidance. High scorers are likely to be considered as good listeners, friendly, non-critical and highly reliable in terms of any commitment that they make.

## LOW

Scores predominantly in the ones and twos ("occasionally" and "almost never") suggest that this individual is aloof or not concerned about customers' issues and might even deliberately distance themselves from them. They are not likely to be aware that customers need sincere advice or support. Even when they find themselves in a more serious conversation, they tend to be oblivious to the depth of a customer's feelings or emotions about an issue.

Low scorers are not usually looked to as sounding boards. Customers with problems or concerns tend to go to others who seem warmer and more accommodating. Low scorers tend to send mixed messages; what they say and what they do are not always the same. Therefore, their relationships with customers are relatively shallow and are restricted to mainly analytical or simple transactional issues.

## ACTION FOR LOW SCORERS

Low scorers need to develop their attentive listening skills and try not to assume that what people say is all of what they mean. Although it is extremely difficult to do in the short term, low scorers need to think more deeply about how customers are feeling as well as what they are saying, and need to reflect on what might be causing these feelings before they comment or respond.

# General Interpretation

Plot your average score for all seven competencies on the chart below. Averages of 4 or more in each competency are "good," scores of 2 to 4 are "worthy of further reflection," and scores less than 2 are "in need of attention" and may need some immediate focus.

**Your Total Customer Service Skills Score**

(Add all seven aggregate scores and divide by seven)

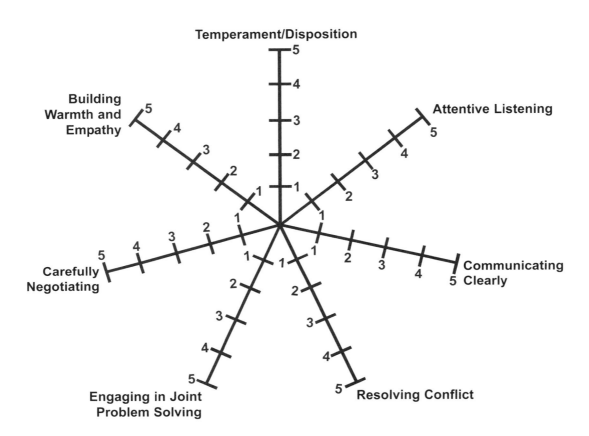

By plotting your average score for each competency on each corresponding axis and then connecting your marks, you create a quick diagrammatic view of your overall Customer Service Skills. The closer your scores are to the center, the better. Efforts to start improving your customer service skills can be concentrated where scores are lowest (generally lower than 3). Although there is no prescriptive strategy that can be recommended for everyone (you must develop your own personal plan), general actions to be taken for each competency are listed on pages 11 and 12.

# Service Skills: Actions

There is no prescriptive strategy that can be recommended for everyone. Each individual must develop their own personal plan. However, here are some general actions for each competency:

| | |
|---|---|
| **Temperament/ Disposition** | • Make a commitment to network widely in order to meet and assist other people; this will help you develop your overall service skills.<br>• Develop the ability to look at issues and situations from the other person's perspective (rather than your own).<br>• Brainstorm and write down as many ways as you can think of to be more helpful or supportive when you are talking with people who ask for your advice and assistance.<br>• Practice comfortably engaging in small talk when you meet with people casually or informally.<br>• Develop an "abundance" mentality in which you offer your help without being asked. |
| **Attentive Listening** | • Find the right kind of climate to listen properly without becoming distracted.<br>• Always try to give people your time and complete attention.<br>• Focus on each customer's particular needs, and listen for as long as possible with minimal interruption.<br>• Play back what you hear from time to time (i.e., by paraphrasing) to demonstrate that you have not let your mind wander.<br>• Learn how to read body language to enhance your listening skills. |
| **Communicating Clearly** | • Give customers time to finish speaking before forming a reply. Maintain your focus, and concentrate as much as possible.<br>• Use the information you gather to carefully plan what you say and how you say it so that your message will be well-received and understood.<br>• Experiment with different communication methods or channels that appeal to a wider range of people.<br>• Keep a log or a diary to record performance feedback or comments on your communication message or style.<br>• Express your views in a clear and concise manner, always explaining why you hold your particular position. |
| **Resolving Conflict** | • Try to quickly demonstrate your genuine and sincere concern that there is a dispute or conflict, and offer to work with the other person to find an acceptable solution.<br>• Use body language and words to help keep the discussion calm and even-tempered.<br>• Spend more time carefully listening to the real or underlying issues in any given conflict situation.<br>• Look carefully for any situational or contextual factors that might be affecting the conflict that you can deal with directly.<br>• Before you respond, put yourself in the customer's shoes and try to see the situation the way it looks to them. |

# Service Skills: Actions

| | |
|---|---|
| **Engaging in Joint Problem Solving** | • Find ways to focus the customer on facts they might have missed.<br>• Suggest tools and methods that might help the customer analyze the problem or issue.<br>• Help customers challenge their old assumptions about outcomes, expectations, etc.<br>• Encourage customers to challenge fixed paradigms or misconceptions that they have about the product or company.<br>• Learn about and try using a variety of problem-solving tools, techniques, and methods for customer service. |
| **Carefully Negotiating** | • Find small and subtle ways to empathize with the customer. Briefly share a personal experience that is similar to theirs, for example.<br>• Explain carefully, calmly, and confidently. Summarize what has been said every few minutes.<br>• Look carefully for areas of agreement (rather than disagreement), and try to build on them when suggesting alternative courses of action.<br>• Share ideas and make proposals positively and enthusiastically.<br>• Always try to look for opportunities to find solutions that represent a "win" for both parties. |
| **Building Warmth and Empathy** | • Commit to being positive, sincere, and open in all your conversations with customers (on the telephone, via e-mail, face-to-face, etc.).<br>• Be sensitive to a person's feelings and emotions as well as their words.<br>• Try to develop a climate of trust with the customer by being as genuine and honest with them as you can.<br>• Make sure that you always carry out your commitments.<br>• Make sure that your deeds match your words, even if it means inconveniencing yourself. |

# Personal Action Planning

Diagnostic instruments take time to complete. If a whole team is involved, it is a significant investment. To derive the most benefit from any diagnostic instrument, at least an equal amount of time should be taken to review the results and engage in some serious individual action planning. Effective action planning requires careful consideration, and it cannot be done in a few short minutes. If we don't back up personal goals with the commitment to achieve them, we set ourselves up for failure.

To help overcome this problem, we have included an action planning tool with the Customer Service Skills Profile on page 10. It asks participants to plot their scores on the "spider diagram" and to then look at which competencies are most in need of development. Once these competency areas are identified, the participant can decide which actions to take to improve those targeted areas.

Whether the individual draws upon these ideas or develops a personal action plan, the improvement actions should be recorded on the template provided on the next page. A copy should be passed to a colleague who agrees to follow up in several weeks or months, checking to see if the individual is sticking to their plan or achieving the results and targets that have been set.

# Personal Action Plan

**My overall score is** [    ]     Date of Action Plan: _____

**The areas most in need of attention (in priority order) and their aggregate scores are:**

SCORE                    COMPETENCY

1. [    ] _____
2. [    ] _____
3. [    ] _____

**My specific plans for becoming more effective in Competency 1 are:**

|  |  | IMMEDIATELY (✔) | By when |
|---|---|---|---|
| Step 1: | _____ | ☐ | _____ |
| Step 2: | _____ | ☐ | _____ |
| Step 3: | _____ | ☐ | _____ |

**My specific plans for becoming more effective in Competency 2 are:**

|  |  | IMMEDIATELY (✔) | By when |
|---|---|---|---|
| Step 1: | _____ | ☐ | _____ |
| Step 2: | _____ | ☐ | _____ |
| Step 3: | _____ | ☐ | _____ |

**My specific plans for becoming more effective in Competency 3 are:**

|  |  | IMMEDIATELY (✔) | By when |
|---|---|---|---|
| Step 1: | _____ | ☐ | _____ |
| Step 2: | _____ | ☐ | _____ |
| Step 3: | _____ | ☐ | _____ |

**In overall terms, I will stop doing or reduce my involvement in:**

1. _____
2. _____
3. _____

**Signature** _____     **Date** _____

# Action Notes

Now that you have assessed yourself on the different customer service skill competencies, you may use the page below to make a number of action notes for yourself. Ideally you should try to focus on areas where your scores are the weakest.

_____

_____

_____

_____

_____

_____

_____

_____

_____

_____

_____

_____

_____

_____

_____

_____

_____

_____

_____

_____

_____

_____

_____

_____

_____

_____

_____

_____

## ABOUT THE AUTHOR

Jon Warner is a professional manager with over 20 years' experience working with multinational companies in the United Kingdom, Europe, the United States, and Australia. He has been the senior staff member in human resources departments, and has held several professional leadership positions with responsibility for large groups of employees. Jon has in recent years been involved in wide-ranging organizational consultancy work and the pursuit of best-practices leadership for such major organizations as Mobil Oil, Quantas, United Energy, Dow Corning, Coca Cola, Barclays Bank, National Bank, Honda, BTR, Gas and Fuel, Air Products and Chemicals, and Caltex.

Jon is managing director of Team Publications PTY Limited, an international training and publishing company committed to bringing practical and fun-to-use learning material to the worldwide training market, such as the One Page Coach® storyboard-based integrated training packages. He holds a master's degree in Business Administration and a Ph.D. in organizational change and learning, and lives and works on Australia's Gold Coast.

## REFERENCES

1. *Service Wisdom,* by Ron Zemke and Chip Bell. Lakewood Books: 1989.
2. *Moments of Truth,* by Jan Carlzon. Harper & Row: 1989 edition.
3. *Keeping Customers for Life,* by Joan Koob Cannie. AMACOM: 1992.
4. *Customers First,* by Denis Walker. Gower Publishing: 1990.
5. *Managing to Keep a Customer,* by Robert L. Deesatnick and Denis H. Hetzel. Josey-Bass Publishers: 1993.
6. *Customer-Driven Quality,* by Richard Whitely. Forum Corporation: 1992.
7. *Communicating with Customers,* by Baden Eunson. John Wiley: 1995.
8. *Resolve Customer Complaints,* by Melody Green (2003).

# Notes

# Notes

# Notes

# Notes

# Notes

# Notes